TAKING ACTION !

INSPIRITING REAL LIFE STORIES,

HOW ORDINARY PEOPLE ARE

'TAKING ACTION !'

& ACHIEVE A HIGHER QUALITY OF LIFE

Table of Contents

Preface

Dear Reader,
Thank you very much for finding your way to this book
and time to read these words. You are about to make
contact with six inspirational real life stories, how
ordinary people are 'Taking Action !' and achieve a
higher quality of life through it. We always have the
choice of watching a series on the couch or thinking
creatively and putting our attention to activities, which
make the world a better place. All stories come from a
point, where the authors decided the second option with
a heightened experience and quality of life as the
rewarding effect.
All authors are very eager people and you will find in
line with a short introduction all information to reach
out and connect. We highly encourage you to do so and
favourably 'Take Action !' together soon!

Enjoy your reading experience,

The Bookwriters Collective

The first story is by April Shwe. April is a very creative woman who is passionate about expressing herself colourfully, as you can see on her welcoming picture:

The colourful picture has been drawn by her, and it is not the only masterpiece she created. When you like to know more about her art and other professions reach out to her on

Linkedin: https://www.linkedin.com/in/april-shwe-aa792073/
Instagram: shwe_artworks
Facebook: https://www.facebook.com/ShweArtworks/

And now, enjoy her colourful expression in words!!

How to help others through self-love and taking action towards your dreams

By April Shwe

Are you the type of person who is constantly putting others' needs before yours? Are you so caring and loving that you go above and beyond what others ask of you? But in doing so do you feel burnt out, exhausted and overwhelmed?

Well that was me in a nut shell, I know what it's like to want to be kind, caring and supportive to others in all areas of my life. But there is a balance of give and take that must be achieved. During my journey of inner reflection and self-discovery; I realized that although I was caring and loving to others, I lacked this care and love for myself. 2018 was the first year in my life I finally started Taking Action towards making things happen for myself. I finally started looking after my health and well-being. For the first time in my life I started getting up at 5am to work out and started eating healthier foods. I started out weighing 68kgs at the beginning of 2018 and before I knew it I was down to 56kgs by October 2018! It wasn't easy to act every day to work out every morning when it's dark outside and you're feeling tired. But once you are in motion towards your goal the easier it is to solidify that habit of Taking Action towards that goal.

Something else I had been neglecting was my passion for Art. I had given it up at the age of 17 years old after being discouraged by my deputy principal from taking Art as my career path. After giving up on it for 8 years, I thought you know what? Life is too short to not live out your passions. So, I started painting part-time after work and on weekends. As scary as it was for me at the time, I started my Art Instagram page and a Facebook page to showcase my artwork. I even took action towards purchasing my first business cards and I was surprised when people started offering to buy my paintings. When I finally started taking actions towards my own wants and needs instead of putting everyone else before me, do you know what happened? Something I thought would be selfish this whole time was actually the most rewarding and profound gift I could've given myself and those around me! My sister started going to the gym regularly being inspired by my commitment to fitness and lost a significant amount of weight. After seeing me reconnect with my passion for art, my partner started thinking about his passions and realized working in a call center isn't what sets his soul on fire. He's now pursuing a path of a fitness coach through being inspired by my actions to live out my passions. Not just my closest family and friends but anyone I came in contact with started re-thinking where they are in life and whether what they are currently doing is truly making them happy or not. By taking action towards my goals I had an impact on others I never knew I could have. Like they say, action speak louder than words. If you want to help others, help yourself first and they will follow in your footsteps.

What a great, light-hearted story of April! Thank you very much for sharing this here with us. To loosen things up, here is a short piece of Maori wisdom to think about deeply:

"Mahia i runga i te rangimarie me te ngakau mahaki"

- With a peaceful mind & respectful heart,
we will always get better results. -

Maori traditions and proverbs are always so enheartening and uplifting, which knows our next author best.

Rebecca Burke has a very profound connection with the Maori culture, although born far apart. She found her link and expresses it in her awe-springing story very beautifully. When you love her story, reach out! Say hi and be astonished about a new amazing connection!

Linkedin: linkedin.com/in/dr-rebecca-burke-6341185a_

Website: www.rebecca-burke.com

Wahine Toa: Step by step… breath by breath ….Setting yourself free

By Rebecca Burke

"I don't love you anymore!"…. these words will forever be stuck in Moana's heart and head. Ten years of marriage at its end in a blink. A void opened up that was ready to swallow her. The Black Hole of pain, shock and anxiety pulled her in and every breath was getting more lifeless.

There she was, alone with two toddlers, no job, no childcare places and totally heartbroken as her husband and love of her life, moved out 3 weeks later. The panic started to take over her life and she was turning in a downwards spiral taking all her energy. She was convinced she would never recover form this. Down and down the spiral went. Moana was crying in hiding and hoping for someone to rescue her. She could not breath and felt the world was closing in on her. Nights went over into days without interruption and the kids eating up her last resources. She knew they needed her more than ever but looking in their eyes, all she could see was their father. The man who once swore to protect her, to be always at her side and that she dreamed of becoming old with. The man that she has experienced so much with, fought for, enjoyed and shared had just stolen himself out of this family. And now Moana was alone. The emptiness in her flat nearly killed her. Torn apart between loneliness and the feeling of hiding, incapable of going outside, incapable of interaction and calling out for help. Instead she pretended to be strong but inside, her world was crumbling and shattered into a million pieces. Breathing became a painful task and she felt that there would never be a fulfilled future again. Moana felt so vulnerable and overwhelmed with emotions like never before in her life.

Anger, fear and pain make us act in strange ways. We are going back on a kind of evolution program that is just focussing on surviving. How do I get through the day? How to protect the children? No long-term planning possible, just surviving in the here and now and coping with the pain. Some people call it depression or PND and even the broken heart syndrome is now a medical term. It is a state of mind and being that many of us have experienced in one way or another and that we all burrowed deep in our hearts and souls.

Six months Moana has spent in this vegetative state of mind and heart till she decided that she needed to take action. In the darkest moments of her life the universe had been kind, sending her the right person to help shift her perspective and igniting her inner fire again. Yes, the virtual and often dishonest world of Facebook has brought someone into Moana's life that reminded her of her inner strength and all the things she had already achieved in her life. She began to see clearer again to be reminded of the things that have been important to her in life. She began to dream again of where she wanted to go and what she wanted to leave behind. Together they developed a vision by looking at the here and now and what Moana's role was and could be. It was a dance of going forth and back between past and future. Gently dipping into the pain and then taking it and trying to transform it or put it in its right place.

At first, there were just words and, step by step, Moana's little life flame began to shine a little bit brighter. Opening herself up to her vulnerability was the key to becoming strong again. But it took courage and trust to admit this. And trust in people was one of the things the pain and betrayal of promise had taken from Moana. Step by step and word by word it appeared to her that there is no shame in feeling like the world is closing in because unexpected turns in life can blow all life-forces out without warning.

Maori people call this life force mauri. Everyone has it and it needs to be protected as it is the essence of every living being. It can grow or can diminish depending our physical and emotional health. Different people in our life can help us to gain new perspectives but in the end we are the guardian of our own mauri. But how to protect and rejuvenate our mauri? With someone that gained her trust and helped her to find a new standing and standing strong behind her, like Maori warriors do in a haka, Moana was able to take little steps moving forward. She stopped the downwards spiral by embracing the love her children gave her every day. She took deep breath every time the emotions took over and began to take care of herself again and to reconnect to friends and new visions for life. Deciding to not feel guilty anymore and face the ugly truth that, the person that she loved most in her life and that she had trusted to the core, had made a decision without consulting her. However, she had to live with the consequences of it.

This truth made her angry and even more vulnerable. But in admitting we have been hurt we open ourselves up for healing. A healing that begins with taking action again and leaving the vegetative state of body and mind. Becoming Wahine Toa and moving forward surrounded by her spiritual warriors that have her back, Moana took action.

Starting from the inside, she began sorting the mess in here life. Gently and step by step she began making plans what needed to be done to move on and to find stability. Her new found "Coach" on this journey called her every day and they just talked about things, feelings and things that needed to be done. With every conversation Moana's mauri retuned a little bit more and the void of loneliness began to fill. After a while, she felt strong enough to take actions that have been visible for the outside too. She began to fight for the things she needed, like childcare place for example. Everything depended on finding a place for the kids so she could go working again and become financially independent. So she opened up in her vulnerable state, visiting places and talking openly about her situation and not feeling ashamed anymore. She even wrote a letter to the major of the town to make sure that this time around she would be considered for two of the scarcest places for the kids. Instead of hiding and closing all doors Moana decide to go the other way. She opened all doors and showed people her vulnerability and, in doing so, letting new things in her life. In a way she became fluid and translucent letting situations and people become part of the journey.

Showing our weakness is something we have been trained to avoid. But showing the shocking truth of pain and anxiety and hurt feelings can be a motivator for others to act honestly and truthful. Moana has been perceived as strong in admitting she felt sad and overwhelmed at times. But in doing so she stayed true to herself and removed all the pressure that was limiting her from action. Her mauri got stronger and stronger and things began to fall into place. And it all began with the first little step to take care of herself again, the reaching out for help and the truthful and honest look at herself and the vision she had for her life. Following that personal vison can make us strong, so strong that we can cope with backslashes and failure and can take far more than we anticipate. This resilience is something we can train and improve. There are many ways to be happy again and many different ways of happiness, but all of these ways only begin with one little action and stepping out of hiding, shame and pain to the space of truthfulness and authenticity: becoming Wahine Toa.

After this connecting stories of so different cultures we, again, refresh our mind with a short quote of profound wisdom:

" Do not figure out big plans at first, but, begin slowly, feel your ground and proceed up and up. "

- Swami Vivekananda

This man, born in India, knew on how to grow as a person and get things done. So does Ankita Dey, who was also born in India and supports entrepreneurs on their journey in New Zealand now.

How she managed to become a widely known person in the Auckland business scene by originating from such a different part of the world, you are about to read. She is so uplifting for all your upcoming projects, reach out to her and stay connected!

Linkedin: https://www.linkedin.com/in/deyankita

As Core member of Innovitas:

http://innovitas.co/about-innovitas/

Board of Trustees of Women Entrepreneurship Centre:

http://wencentre.org.nz/team/

Feel the fear, act on it

My journey of how I made my dream come true

By Ankita Dey

This is the story of a young enthusiastic migrant of how she embraced a new culture, overcame her fears, and made her childhood dream come true.

As a shy young girl, I spent most of my early years observing life rather than actively participating in whatever it offered. Being an introvert who would feel comfortable in talking to only a specific set of people, expressing my views and feelings always felt like a hurdle, big enough to prevent me from climbing it often.

From my early childhood, I had big dreams in life and just didn't want to settle for an ordinary one. But for that, I had to come out of my shell. One of the most valuable advices that constantly resonate in my head was something that my grandfather gave me when I was 11 years old – 'Feel the fear and act on it; don't let it eat you out'. Since then I made sure never to look back. I joined all possible student committees, took as many group responsibilities as I could, because I knew the only way to come out of my comfort zone was to be able to talk, indulge in networking and meeting new people in these groups. I finally managed to take a plunge in the social world and could confidently talk to others.

But as we all know the journey of life is not always smooth; it presents you twists and turns with every passing moment. And that makes living so much fun and interesting, right?

At 27 years of age, I got married and moved to New Zealand and joined my husband. Coming from India, the people, the culture here was so new and different. It would be safe to say that not having enough exposure of how the cultures were outside of my home country came up as a cultural shock. This reminded me of my time as a 10 year old girl from India who was very comfortable in her own circle, but diffident to talk to new people. Guess what, this was the déjà-vu moment. The only person I knew in this new country was my husband who would be at work for a decent time of the day.

It was at this time that the golden words of my grandfather gave me the courage and showed me the path. I needed to create a new satyr – 'a story of empowerment to encourage myself and others like me'. But the lingering questions that I had in my head were – where do I start from? Whom should I talk to? How should I set that first stepping stone? The only way that I knew of moving forward was to start connecting with people. I opened my laptop, did a detailed research on the startup system in NZ for a week and sent emails to over 100 people in the New Zealand startup ecosystem. And as terrified as I was wondering of what they would think of this approach from an amateur like me, I knew that I did the right thing.

At some point in my childhood, I had started to feel very strongly that I had an inclination towards having my own entity. *Something that I would want to build with passion. Something that I could call my own.* It was a dream that was always on my mind. I truly felt that I had the potential and caliber to do it, and with one step in the right direction, I would embark on this dream-fulfilling journey.

Two days passed by and there was not even a single response to my mails. After a few days, one fine day I got a response from the founder of Women Entrepreneurship Centre (WEC), Auckland. We met over a coffee and I was so excited to share my ideas and my passion - I didn't get time to take even a single sip. And today I am one of the Board of Trustees of the same organization. Along with the amazing team at WEC, I got a chance to guide and support over 15 women entrepreneurs, and I feel so proud to share that a few of them have an established business today. What could be better than a start with guiding and encouraging women eager to develop their own business? Reminds me of my childhood dream where I wanted to build my own business. One advice I always shared with them was – Don't let the fear eat you out. If you have got some business idea in your mind, just start working on it!

Since then I never stopped. I have been to countless meetups and workshops to interact with more and more people. This was the only way I could make myself comfortable among new people and the new culture. I knew from my own experience how bright and wonderful it feels to be able to connect with people and develop something with them, for them. Today I have successfully established Founders' Lab in New Zealand and have organized over 15 domestic and international events and workshops. Feedbacks like – 'It lights up my fire again when I meet you' and 'yesterday's discussions around the capabilities of what I could achieve with my business kept me up all night' just makes my day. I have business partners with a network of over 4500 business professionals. I have also mentored 3 women led startups in the last 18 months. Along with my business partners, we have recently started supporting university students, the budding entrepreneurs of tomorrow.

It gives me immense pleasure to realize how the world has opened up for me finally. As an entrepreneur I have been able to share my story with people from various other countries. A lot of these people have told me how they resonate with my story. I follow a simple mantra – 'If you stand back analyzing the best way to do something, you'll end up standing there. Just do it. Keep learning and moving towards the next goal'. Trust me, the guilt of not being able to do something takes a lot more energy than just getting it done!

I'm very grateful for the way things have turned out for me. Today, I'm running a successful business. And more than anything, I'm happy and looking forward to a bright future.

After this encouraging story of a woman succeeding through all odds, we revitalize by this quote and title of a book, which the following author highly credits for his happy way of living:

- Nino Anders

The book by Nino Anders equipped Sascha Të Light with an optimistic outlook to life.

He is bold, full of energy and goes for what life presents him, by being aware and sensitive to the guiding feeling and voice inside. He has written a couple of inspirational humorous books and shares one story here with us. Reach out to him, connect and interact on your preferred platform!

Amazon Author Page:

https://www.amazon.com/author/saschatelight

Linkedin: https://www.linkedin.com/in/sascha-të-light-582262106

The freeway to success

By Sascha Të Light

(excerpt from SEXY HEALTHY LIVING)

" In order to attend many events I was interested in, I did this following move, which I am sure, you will love. It is a big secret and I think it is an amazing discovery. Since I was partly representing companies at their events as their Brand Ambassador, which I did for Amazon and Google as examples, I knew, that the organizers always appreciated the help and support of some people. The attendees had to be checked in, welcomed and sometimes introduced to the event. When I found events, which were really expensive, like the *"PwC Herald Talk"* or an event called *"Success Squared with Gary Vee"*, I simply wrote to the Facebook-page, if they would appreciate some support for their event. At both mentioned events, the organizers got back to me and were really happy about my offering. At the second one, I furthermore got offered to invite more people to volunteer along with me as well. I brought five other people along. Which I found was an amazing win-win situation, I got in for free and even appeared as someone "special" at the event through being part of the crew. I got the benefits usually only the very high paying attendees got, a picture with the stars. Especially the Gary Vee event was amazing for several purposes. JT Foxx was speaking at this event as well. If you did not know JT Foxx yet, he brands himself as the

"World Number One Wealth Coach". He was the most successful stage-selling speaker and used to sell his follow-up weekend event or training course for five thousand Dollars. He was statistically proven the one, who got the most people to take action and bought his offerings. I knew him from one of his free events before, where he almost got me to buy something of him. I found it incredible, how he built up a feeling inside me, that I really had to have his program. And because he made his offer *"exclusive"* to the first sixteen customers (what a joke), people were really running in the middle of his presentation to get to the table and be one of the lucky *"sixteen"*. The first time, I was truly very close. He had a very structured, honest and direct way of speaking, which appealed to me, to others not at all. He was very aware of that and I appreciated his truthfulness. In line with his generosity, as you will find out soon.

At the Gary Vee event he was also presenting and selling his upcoming two day seminar in Auckland for five thousand Dollars. Because I was part of the crew, I was standing at the table where the people came to fill out their order form to buy. Once they filled everything out, I handed them over a small piece of paper with a congratulations-note and online login-details to register for the upcoming event. I got the idea to take a picture of these sheets and registered for the event myself. To my surprise, I got confirmed. I was not one hundred percent sure, if I would be able to attend, still I kept it in my mind and calendar. As the day of the event came closer, I received an email from the organization. They were asking, how I got confirmed, because there was no payment to my name. I told them the truth, and they said, that I was not able to attend.

I thought: *"Aahhh, well, nice try."* It was fine. And I kept the date in my mind.

It took place on a Sunday and Monday and I had nothing else going on that Sunday. So I decided to go there anyway and try to get in personally. As JT Foxx was a business person and encouraged to professionally suit up with tie and business shoes, I exactly did that. I borrowed a black suit with a red tie from one of my friends and went there in this attire. I arrived at the hotel, where the seminar was about to happen. There were two men sitting in front of the door. I walked up to them and showed them my email of confirmation. They looked in their system and got back to me, saying:

"Sorry, Mister, you are not in the system. Did you pay for it or did someone else paid for you, since you are confirmed?"

I told them the true story, that I was part of the crew at the Gary Vee event and helped selling today's seminar. I registered and got confirmed.

"Well, we can not let you in, except we get five thousand Dollars of you."

Ah, well, I understood. I left the hotel and thought that this was obviously right of them. And still, there was a feeling inside me, to hold on. I was already dressed up. I decided to go to a second entry of the hotel and to wait there. I was already well connected in the Auckland business scene and had some good friends, also on Facebook, who bought JT's programs before and were very well acquainted with him. I saw him posting underneath a post of a friend of mine. And I thought:

"Well, I can write him myself". I took a picture, describing everything honestly and truthfully and hoped,

that he would get back to me.

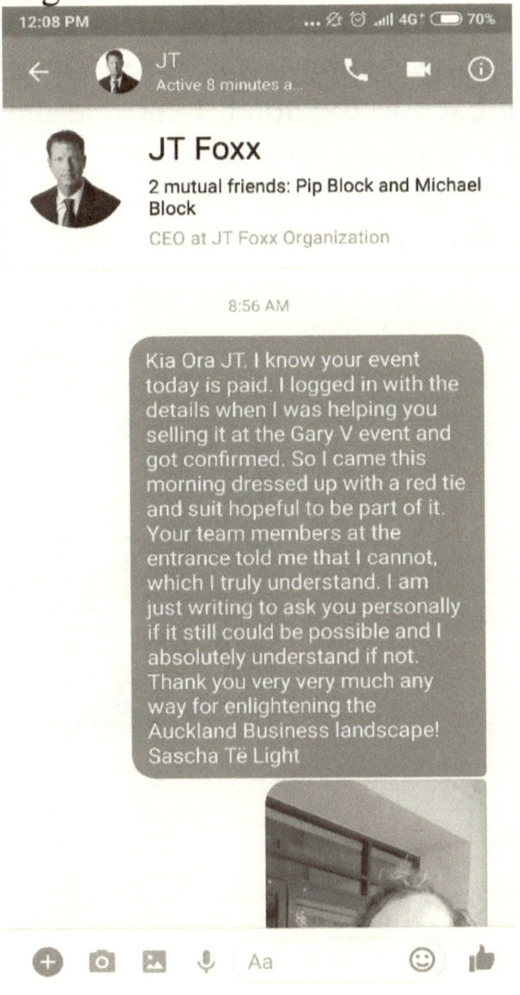

My chat history with JT Foxx

I waited for ten minutes, the seminar already started and I thought, it probably was too late now. I left from the hotel and walked the street a bit up. I was already content with myself, to have put in a lot of energy and effort. The notification light of my smartphone lit up and he truly saw my message! And he replied! Saying

yes, that I was able to attend! To his five thousand Dollars Seminar! I was so happy, really, I was actually so surprised, how happy I was. I felt so exuberant and was running back to the hotel. I showed the two men at the entrance my phone with the message of JT and they allowed me to get in, saying perplex:
"I have no idea what you did, have fun."

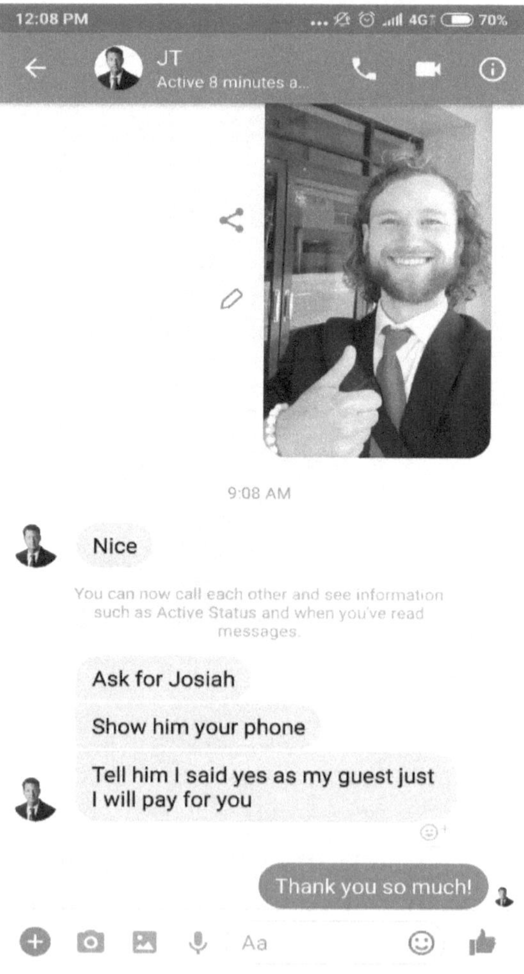

JT Foxx's reply

Now I was sitting in this five thousand Dollars seminar and it was really amazing. The first day was devoted to simply sharing knowledge, the basic business mindset and the characteristics of successfully operating in the business world. I learnt so many things, although the main thing was simply to be in the presence of JT and the other speakers. There was always such a transmission of energy happening, that I felt very lifted just through being there. I found a plethora of gold-nuggets in JT's views.

Very good, this was a very good day. Since I did not know about the outcome of this day, I already had confirmed to a film-shoot on Monday, so I was not able to attend the second day.

By sharing this story with you, dear Reader, I like to encourage you especially in the following highlighted ways:

First, it is always good to attend events. Especially volunteering at events you passionately enjoy, is a double win-win, because you get more easily in contact with a lot of people, who have similar passions to you. In addition to benefits, which usually are reserved for people, who have to pay a lot of money for them.

Second, persistency is one of the big keys to life. I received a *"No"* via email, I received a *"No"* from the men in front of the seminar. I kept going on, kept going on persistently for the anticipated outcome. And this attitude applies to everything, either a business event, or the business itself, where we continuously have to keep on going and the longer we keep on going, the more we succeed. Success is the guaranteed and automatic consequence of persistently taking action. Which also applies to the dating world. When there is a woman, or a man, we deeply feel in love with and he or she somehow does not see it from the first moment as we do, simply keeping on going, maybe even for months, is a good strategy! Of course, always with respecting if there is a strong, hard *"No"*. Especially women love this persistency of a longer period of time because this makes all of us appreciate:

"Uh, this guy/girl is really going for what he/she feels and never gives up. How amazing and rare."

And third, honesty. I could have said other things in my emails, to the men, to JT, which I am sure of, would have never gotten me into the room. I chose to be honest and truthful during all time. And I am absolutely certain, that this keeps my soul being pure and allows me to live a life of outstanding, extraordinary events and experiences. "

Awesome, after this journey into the freeway of success, revitalize with this eminent quote:

> *"When I say or do something, I do it."*
> – Eminem

Kelly Smith also gets things done. Whatever life presents to her, she embraces it and moves forward to the direction of her happy place.

Without further talking about it, her is she, revealing it herself. Connect with her on her online presences:

Writers platform:
https://writers.work/bluerosecopywriting

Linkedin: https://www.linkedin.com/in/kelly-smith-b4753a162

<u>Motivation</u>

by Kelly Smith

I stare out the scratched window and wonder if its normal to dread five o clock.

1992. It's gloomy this early in the day in coastal Connecticut. Everything seems grey, even the graffiti on the freeway underpasses.

I'm twenty years old, and as I curl into the hard plastic seat of the public bus, I realize... there's no point to this. To any of this. To me.

My day is set. After work, I'll go home to the war zone that's my house. I'll pray not to see my father's car in the driveway. If it's there... I'll go inside anyway. I don't have a choice.

I hope it won't be bad today...

I feel like I'm suffocating.

And that's the moment I decide that I don't want to live like this anymore... I have a choice to make.

Blink.

1993. I'm in the back of the viewing room at my grandfather's funeral. My baby sister is squirming in my arms. Thankfully, she's not crying.

My mother is devastated, silently weeping off to the side. Her father has died, but her siblings aren't welcoming her into their pew. She hadn't quite made it to see Grandpa before he died... She'd been half an hour too late. My father had delayed her on purpose, forbidden her from going without him, and he'd deliberately been late.

My aunts and uncles don't understand what it's like, to be us... and they don't care.

My father is at the funeral. I'm not sure if it's just more of his cruelty or if he honestly thinks he's helping. Either way, I avoid him.

I stand there, rocking the baby so my mother doesn't have that to worry about, and I realize that I have to make a choice. It's the same choice I made a year ago. *Stay* or *go.*

Live or die?

For a year, I've been planning my escape.

It takes a while to figure out where I'll go. I've been researching job markets, crime rates, quality of life, public transportation... everything I can think of.

I won't go anywhere my father knows anyone. I know I can't stay on the Eastern Seaboard. I can't be anywhere that's familiar.

I've put a deposit on a small apartment in Denver, Colorado. I've only seen it in pictures.

I have a plane ticket. It'll be my first flight.

But then Grandpa dies a month before I'm set to run.

I grieve twice. Once for him, and once for me... How can I leave my mom now? How can I add to her grief? I know how my father will react when he finds out what I've done. How can I do that to her?

How can I leave my sister? She'll never know me.

The hardest thing I've ever done is choosing to leave.

Blink.

It's 1996. I'm talking with a young man over email. I don't even suspect that I'm in love... until one day I get home and I realize that I've been smiling ever since I read his last email to me... and that was four hours ago.

He invites me to meet his parents. In California.
And just like that, I have to choose all over again. Stay where I'm safe and where I'm building a life on my own, or take a chance on this earnest, loving young man.
This choice shouldn't be tougher than my first one, but it is. I feel safe for the first time in my life, and I like that. A lot. Do I really want to take another big risk?
In the end, I choose to take the second biggest chance of my life...
(*We marry four years later.*)

Blink.
It's 2017. I have a job as an educational aide at my children's school.
I love all the kids I work with. I don't even mind recess duty... it lets me walk the playgrounds and talk to the kids who're lonely, bullied, or different. They smile when they see me coming because they know I listen. I care.
It's absolutely the best year of my working life. It's my dream job.

Blink.
In 2018 I lose it.
I don't know what to do. I just know that I have a school bill to pay and I need another job. *Now.*
It's tempting to pull the blankets over my head and pretend nothing happened, but I've never been able to do nothing.
I know that I need a job that works around school and my children's schedule. I absolutely refuse to take time away from them.
I finally take my love of words, my love for helping

people, and the storytelling skills I've never used outside of a classroom, and I create Blue Rose Copywriting.

I'm thrilled and terrified at the same time.

My company is in its infancy, but I really love what I do. I'm making a difference for my clients. Several of them have become friends.

If I'd stayed in my comfortable bubble and not risked acting on my dream, I'd never have any of this.

So here's what I want you to take away from this story...

- A bad situation should only be temporary... It's not meant to be your whole life. *Endure... but move on*.

- Be intentional and thoughtful about how, why and when you take action, but *act*.

- Good often comes in disguise. A good thing doesn't always look the way you think it will. That doesn't make it any less good. Be open to the possibilities.

- The truth. *You were made for joy*. You deserve joy. But joy needs you to be willing and receptive to it.

- *Above all, have faith*. Nothing's a guarantee. Faith lets you act even though the outcome might be fuzzy. Have faith in your business, in your decision... in you.

I promise you... you're worth it.

2019 – Blue Rose Copywriting

How interesting life can be! An ever changing adventure and in case of any situations, always remember this wise Zen-Buddhist wisdom from Japan:

" It will pass...
There is the story of a Zen master to whom a disciple comes. He has such great difficulties in meditation, he says to the master. His back hurts, his legs hurt and every now and then he even falls asleep. 'It will pass,' the Zen master tells him. Weeks later the disciple comes back and is completely euphoric. He was doing so well, the disciple reported. He is wide awake, full of peace and joy and fully present. To which the master replies:

'This will pass.' "

- from Japan

And as the final founding author in our bookwriters collective, Latisha Pinnington delights us with her encouragement.

Be prepared to gain a deep insight to life and feel inspired to think in a new, universal way. When you like to have further conversations in that regards, reach out!

Linkedin:

https://www.linkedin.com/in/latisha-pinnington-bb5030126

A Spiritual Awakening
A Call to Action

By Latisha Pinnington

"When we admit to ourselves that we are a unique being of a greater plan we see beauty in unexpected places," LT. I was awakened to the situation, that we as humans face a global epidemic of extinction and our planet is desperately in need for change. This hit me hard. I had been asleep, brainwashed, self-absorbed, out of my head. This was an overwhelming feeling of emotion, I felt like my whole life had been one big lie, made up, not real. This started a chain of events which flowed like clockwork. Some call it the Power of Attraction, Universal Flow, Fate, Destiny, God, whatever the semantics, this was a sign I needed to 'take action' somehow. I wanted to scream out at the top of my lungs, WAKE UP !!!! We are all dreaming !!!! It's time, we need to shift and move before we wake up and it's all gone. This awakening took me to Australia and even the USA several times and I was introduced to global thought leaders and great people making great changes. I had this intuition, this inner voice, I couldn't sleep, work, do anything. It consumed me. The Universe had been waiting for me. Waiting for what? A call to action, to make changes in my life so I could fulfil what my purpose was. And what was this purpose? To shift the awareness of the human race. What awareness? To raise the energy levels of the people. Energy, what energy and what people? The energy that we are here to solve the global issues we face today and we will succeed. That energy. The energy that tells our spirits and raises hope to the everlasting truth that humanity can survive, we will solve the issues we face, and to never give up, the answers are there, waiting. I believe I am writing this now as part of my purpose. To help you wake up, to become aware, to raise the energy levels of those around you. The more we share what we are experiencing the more we find others like us. That whatever you are going through, someone else has too. That what you seek, others are also. That answers have been found, others are already aware and working on it. Join in or get left behind. Together we are stronger, together we will prevail and together we can make a difference. Every single one of us. The Universe doesn't care what colour you are, what race, where you were born, how much money you have. All it cares about is survival. Our survival. So have some faith, give back to it even more love, awaken others, and the more we do, the more love we share, the more energy we raise and the more forgiving we are of ourselves, the Universe will be so in return. It is time we take action and stand up for truth, for justice, for the human race, the time is NOW.

First Update

Dear Reader,

we started this experiment green, with nothing big in our mind. This has changed and the idea grew to expand 'The Bookwriters Collective'.

We came up with the idea, that eager, kind-hearted and well-intented authors can be found everywhere in the world. Therefore it became one milestone of this book to feature one or more people out of every country in the world at one stage.

So far we have Germany, New Zealand, India and the United States represented. We are honoured and proud to share the stories of amazing authors from Pakistan, Switzerland, Egypt, Australia, Spain and the United States for a second time through this first update with you.

And we start now with the benevolent story of Mariya. Mariya was born in Karachi in Pakistan. Life treated her well in Karachi and she got to fulfil herself as IT professional with the connection to the field of human resources. Enjoy her very poetic way of 'Taking Action !'

You can find and connect with Mariya Gul Khand easily here:

Linkedin:
https://www.linkedin.com/in/mariyagulkhand2019

Swirling Waters and tumbling waves

By Mariya Gul Khand

Swirling waters and tumbling waves, this is the turbulent, tempestuous condition of my mind. As I contemplate on where the waves have been taking me, suddenly I find myself landing on an Island. As I move on, I meet with a lot of familiar faces in this unfamiliar place: anger, hope, anxiety, bliss, melancholy, love, hatred, jealousy and faith. But who were they? A part of me, perhaps. But where did they come from? And where was I?

Alas! I found the truth. The truth or mystery? Indeed, a dreamy world is a secret; where "I", yes, "I am everything". Just like dreams, I prefer to live in my own thoughts, because I strongly believe that our mind can create anything and make everything possible. The key is letting my mind wander so that my intuitive abilities can generate ideas.

When I'm dreaming, I feel like I'm watching a movie that plays on the screen of my mind. What I watch there, determines the kind of life I live and the best thing about this movie is that I get to direct it, and that's totally free of cost. I'm the actor, the director and the producer here. I am not dependent on anyone, and that's what the most empowering thing about it is!

The reality on the other hand is painful and there are a lot of questions that my mind asks while I'm awake in this world. There is so much that I seek for, and try to find. Until I find them in real life, I'd prefer to stay asleep, while you may enjoy my poetry that lists the details of my unattainable goals, for indeed not every inspirational story is a success story.

I seek to find reality in shattered dreams,
I seek to find light in the sky's hidden beams.

I seek to find honesty in the markets of deception,
I seek to find truth in the torments of manipulation.

I seek to find diversity where prejudice is an exception,
I seek to find inclusion where there is no point of rejection.

I seek to find equality where there is no discrepancy,
I seek to find empathy when faced with an emergency.

I seek to find hearts free from the disease of <u>narcissism</u>,
I seek to find brains that are not struck by bitter <u>cynicism</u>.

I seek to find eyes that to me are a mirror of my honest reflection,
I seek to find hands that don't drive me towards the wrong direction.

I seek to find people, who are not involved in blatant backbiting,
I seek to find a way to share what I strongly believe in, by writing...

After this colourful story we shake things a bit up and be remembered by the words of Siddartha Gautama:

"Yourself, in line with every one in the whole universe deserves your love and affection."

These words keep inspiring generation after generation after generation. This is what we and especially Marwa intends as well.

Marwa Madkour originates from the warmhearted heat of Egypt. She shares her passion of teaching English as her second language. She mastered the skill of intercultural communications with her connection to the ancient civilization of Egypt, as you can see on her amazing representative picture:

Please reach out and connect with her on LinkedIn:

https://www.linkedin.com/in/marwa-madkour

And Facebook:
https://m.facebook.com/englishpyramid.eg/
https://m.facebook.com/MarwaMadkour33/

Zeinab

By Marwa Madkour

She was crying and tears made her amazingly dark eyes sparkle more than usual. They were glowing like two black moons; they were radiating with intelligence and sadness. She knew how lonely she was, but she didn't know whether she was crying because her classmates were mocking her for not being able to speak Arabic properly or because she lost her mother a few months ago. She couldn't stop thinking about her caring and loving mother who wanted her to have the best education ever; that's why she enrolled her daughter in a French Jesuit school that was well-known at the time for being so keen on nurturing good manners and etiquette. But now, everything was gone and every beautiful dream was gone just like her mother.

Her father thought that it was unnecessary for his daughter to learn French, especially when it made her struggle while speaking in her mother tongue. Thus, the decision was made to move her to an Arabic school where she struggled to structure Arabic sentences properly or pronounce standard Arabic correctly. It was very harsh to be laughed at while still grieving her beloved mother, but she didn't give up. She was only five years old, but she was smart enough to know that her world had changed forever and that she had to be strong and be able to cope.

She tried to take care of her two-year-old brother as

well, but that was no easy thing to do. So, her father decided to get married again for the sake of his little children as it was almost impossible to take care of them alone. It was extremely hard for her to understand how a stranger could take the place of her mother and on the other hand it was so difficult for the stepmother to love and support two children who were not her own. It was a tough journey they all had to go through.

Years went by and that little girl became an amazingly beautiful lady. She was thoughtful and angelic which made it extremely hard not to be admired and loved by everyone; even by her stepmother. Ironically, that crying girl, who was teased for her poor Arabic, had become an accomplished Arabic language teacher herself. She had never forgotten that situation, but instead of feeling sorry for herself, she turned it into motivation. She eventually excelled at Arabic and outdid herself. She was that unique type of teachers who would gather all pupils struggling with reading and writing and those who had learning difficulties and by the end of the school year, they would become among the top students. This magnificent change got her overwhelmed with joy each year.

Let me take a huge leap in time, three decades had passed through which she had been a faithful wife and a devoted mother of three daughters. Professionally, she had become a successful school principal who earned the respect of everybody whom she worked with. She had never stopped missing her mother and sought comfort in her girls by giving them everything she wished to have with her own mother. She was a living proof that the old Latin idiom "**nemo dat quod non habet**" is not true since she could always give what she did not have; motherly love.

Unfortunately, she had to go through another loss; this time it was her husband. He had been perfectly healthy, but in a blink of an eye was gone to his last resting place. The unpredictability of sudden death doubles the anguish and triples the heartache. She was about to fall apart, then she thought of her girls and was determined to be strong since she knew that she was everything they had. For the second time, she was alone in this world or at least *Zeinab* felt this way, with only God by her side. Yes! Her name was Zeinab, which is the name of a beautiful aromatic tree, and in her warm shades lived the ones she loved the most; her daughters.

Let's take a second big leap in time, twenty years had been over in which she played the roles of a mother, father, mentor and friend for her daughters; and she did this incredibly well. She had been through a lot of hard times, but she kept standing tall no matter what. By that time, she had helped two of her daughters in their marriage preparations and even helped them with their first babies. She was too old for this effort; she pushed herself to the limit and did it for their sake though. Then, she had been living alone with her younger daughter who then had been engaged for more than a year and was working on her wedding arrangements and soon wedding day was to be set. Later on, in July 2018, her daughters grievously received the worst news ever; Zeinab was diagnosed for a vicious type of liver cancer and at a very advanced stage. They couldn't dare tell her the truth, so they took the decision to hide this reality.

It had been a bumpy road where all doors had been knocked, but there was not one flicker of hope for her recovery. They decided to quickly settle on a date for her daughter's wedding ceremony as they wanted her to be there on that day. As usual, Zeinab did everything in her power so that every single detail was taken care of. Those were indescribable days; they were researching and fighting for hope for their mother, praying to God that she doesn't suffer, working on the wedding preparations, trying to ignore all those who were nothing but a huge disappointment, and the hardest part was to act as if there was nothing wrong and to actually feel happy.

Thanks to Allah, the big day had come and she was there with them watching the beautiful bride get ready and go down the flowery stairs to dance with her groom. She had always prayed for that day. Everybody was excited and I was very grateful that she was present.

Fifteen days later, in October 2019, she was gone. She went to her better place and to the mercy of her creator. My mother is gone, but not forever; for I know there comes a day when I will hold you in my arms and read you this story myself. I am still moving on as you want me to be and I can still hear your voice in my ears telling me "Stay strong!" I still hear you asking me to have a seat so that I don't get tired while you were lying on your hospital bed. You were an island of selflessness in a self-centered world.

You will always be my greatest role model and my ultimate inspiration. You taught me how we can survive every difficulty, how to be grateful for all that we have, how to have control over our destiny, and most importantly how to accept our fate patiently. "I'm wholeheartedly proud to be your daughter."

I dedicate this story to you and to every strong woman out there in the world.

Written by

Marwa Madkour
21 June, 2019.
Giza, Egypt

After this profound rememberance of our connection to our parents and the gift they gave us to be here on earth, we are reminded with another profound thought of ancient egyptian wisdom:

"Exuberance is a great stimulus towards action, although inner light grows in silence and concentration."

From the heat of Egypt we switch into the teachings of the mountains in Europe. Isabella Peintner was born in Switzerland, gained experience in a multitude of different countries and is today your go to expert for consulting in software licensing and managing sales in this particular field.

Also her writing skills are of exceptional quality, as you are   about   to   read   now.

Connect with her through her LinkedIn profile:

From Munich to Zürich – sunsets, beaches and Gangsta Rap

By Isabella Peintner

When I was just a little girl around 4 years of age I told my mother that I wanted to emigrate and that I needed her jewelry so I could buy a plane ticket. I always had a dream of foreign places where there was more sun and fun than where I lived. I had a small 5m² room and the room of my brother Christian, who was a year and a half my senior, was the double size - that was not fair! In addition, my parents were arguing over everything and nothing all day and they spoke Bavarian dialect which sounded rude to me. I preferred proper high German. I didn't like the long winters without any sunshine and I didn't like my pale skin that got red when it was really cold. I always used to stare out my window and wonder about other fun places that I could go explore in the world. Several years later I had studied the world map and spent some of my free time studying the capital cities of the major countries in all continents. I had also made up my mind that I would have to learn a minimum of 6 foreign languages in this life. My decision was set to emigrate to a foreign country far away, one day.

During my teens I was heavily influenced by several TV shows that had conquered living rooms all over the world, such as "Knight Rider" and "Baywatch". Beautiful suntanned people were smiling on TV screens, some with red life savers jumping in the Pacific, looking all happy and healthy. Coming home after school I was usually fighting with my brother over all kinds of stuff. We argued about the TV remote control, whose favourite music would set the tone in the kitchen and who would get the bigger half of the Watermelon my mother had cut in halves. We both loved that fruit like nothing else! One thing we didn't fight about was tuning into our favorite TV shows right after school ended around 1 pm. We both loved the drama stories around blondes in bikinis, sun and beach. Everyone seemed to smile there, look good and obviously Malibu was the place to be! I started to wonder if California would be a nice place to live.

I was a girly girl when I was young and a ballet dancer since the age of 6. When my brother got his first tennis racket I wanted one, too, and I quit Ballet. For the next years we both practiced tennis every day and by the age of 18 we both reached a near pro level competing in major clubs in Munich and in tournaments all over Bavaria. Around the time I graduated from high school and one of my brothers tennis buddies had just come back from spending a year in the US. He broke the news that studying in a US college with a tennis scholarship was an amazing experience. He put us in contact with his coach and shortly thereafter everything was set up for both of us to study and play tennis abroad. Here we come USA! We flew into Atlanta, Georgia to reach our final destination Augusta. It was the home of the famous Masters golf pro tournament, but I had never heard of this city before and I was not interested in golf at that time!

Life as a student athlete was totally cool. We were living in the dorms and my roommates were two black girls. They spoke an accent that I could hardly understand but I found it a really cool experience. Their cooking was so different and they would spend hours in front of the mirror to style their hair. In the tennis team we were a dozen international young women and men coming from countries such as Sweden, South Africa, Germany and Armenia. After school we practiced tennis on the courts everyday and during the weekends we would travel with the team in a VW bus to compete against schools in Florida, Georgia, South Carolina and even Alabama. I loved the positive atmosphere on campus, the tennis competition and seeing new places when being on the road all the time. Living life as a student athlete was the best thing that had happened to me ever!

Georgia had never been on my mind before and I never liked the large insects and roaches that were creeping and flying in such a humid weather such as Georgia in summer. Malibu beach was still a dream. If I could make it to America, I could also make it to California after all! During my first successful season in Augusta I decided to give it a shot to find a school at the West Coast. I found a book in the library with a list of all colleges and athletic departments and randomly dialed up tennis coaches in Southern California. Around a hundred phone calls later and some paperwork following, some good bye dinners and a sweet summer break in Munich, I found myself in Los Angeles later that summer for the start of my first fall semester in California. I had been offered a full scholarship to Cal State Northridge in the San Fernando Valley, a place around 40 minutes north of Los Angeles and 40 minutes east of Malibu. I bought myself a surfboard and checked it in along with my tennis rackets. Never had I seen such a spread area of lights and squares than when I was approaching LAX airport by place. This place was huge! I lived in Northridge for the next four years and it was a truly fantastic experience. The temperature was at 40 degrees nearly each day and I loved the heat and the sun. I went to school with inline skates like they were doing on Venice beach. I usually had a gallon of water can in my hand because tennis practice was at noon from 1pm to 4pm daily. I would get very thirsty and drank a lot to stay hydrated. I wore colorful shorts and tank tops every day and my skin was always tanned. For the first time in my life going to the gym became a routine and I have never ever been so fit before. My hair had turned blonde from the sun and when I walked down the street random men turned their head and said : *"Daaaammmm girllllll"*.

During my time in Northridge I dated an American Eritrean student few years my senior. His family had migrated to the U.S. when he was around 10 years old and even though he was still close to his African roots he was really into U.S. mainstream culture. Rap had been really popular in the 90s all over the world and I admired his ability to understand the lyrics and rap along. We shared an apartment, adopted a few stray cats from the street and watched the orange red sunsets every night from our balcony facing west. Songs from "2Pac" and "Snoop Doggy Dog" were blasting out our window. Now I was not only a successful tennis player and an A-student in my favorite subject psychology but I also learnt all about rap music, African roots and life as an interracial couple in the 90s. Sometimes we would draw all eyes on us. I didn't care and I found it funny that people would be surprised that a German successful tennis player would date a skinny yet teddy style black man that was working at a gas station at night to afford his college tuition. Living with a boyfriend who loves good music, rapped me love songs on my answering machine and treated our cats better than himself was just such a present sent from god.

When I graduated with my Bachelors in psychology, my life was about to take a radical change. My soon to be ex-boyfriend moved to Las Vegas and I moved back to Germany because my tennis scholarship had ended with the completion of my degree. I moved back to Munich and experimented with several internships. I studied Spanish in Ecuador, taught tennis in holiday clubs around Europe and finally decided to move back to the USA, where people were more outgoing and positive than I had found them in Europe. I found a scholarship as an assistant tennis coach in West Virginia that would allow me to pay for my MBA. I continued my travel lifestyle finding jobs in Pittsburgh, San Diego and later in Berlin, Germany, where I kickstarted my career in Sales at an American U.S. Software company, Oracle. I later worked for Volkswagen and finally headed for a better opportunity to Bern and Zürich, where I currently reside.

Living abroad has become my lifestyle since I had decided on that as a young girl. Today I am fluent in six languages and lately I have been keen on adding number seven. I have dated and married men from foreign countries and if I am not living as an expatriate, I am probably working in an international company. Having had a myriad of experiences and friendships with people from all over the world shaped my personality more than anything. I consider myself a very open-minded and culturally flexible person who engages with everyone easily. Some of my best friends live in Los Angeles and they have always said to me that L.A. is the place to be. When you live in LA you don't need to travel the world because the world travels to you. That is true! As an explorer, I had to choose the traveling part. Lately, Switzerland has become my home and I have built an amazing network and live a good lifestyle after some years. Regardless, at the whim of a moment, everything can change again. Australia, South Africa and South East Asia have been on my mind lately.

What an eminent story of how life gifted Isabella with this inner calling, which turned out to be real in such an exuberant way. Amazing! Maybe Isabella listened closely to the words of the famous Swiss psychoanalyst Carl Gustav Jung:

"I am not what happened to me, I am what I choose to become."

Australia was already on Isabella's mind, so no we switch into the story of 'Taking Action!' by Jimmy Pan. Sydney is home to Jimmy for a long time. Here he feels comfortable and convenient to fulfill his and the life of his family. He is doing very well, as an active trade manager for financial traders, as person with a huge social supporting network and presentation and as a father, with a strong care for his children, which is so important in life.

Be amazed by his courageous and insight-rich story on how he became, what he is today.

Connect with Jimmy Pan on LinkedIn:
https://www.linkedin.com/in/jimmycpan

A Relentless Mindset

By Jimmy Pan

I've always been an optimistic person who is not shy of taking risks and believes that everything happens for a reason. Until I took a big risk and made a mistake. A big mistake, that put my mental strength to the test like nothing ever had before. And I was failing.

So this is my story of how I changed my path.

Following a chance encounter with a long-time friend whom I had not seen in years, I discovered what Joseph Campbell calls "the elixir" when he tells the story of the hero's journey.

I was able to make that pivotal mental shift; to recover from hitting rock bottom both mentally and physically, find my purpose, fight for a one-in-a-million job, and win. To come out feeling worthy, and make an impact.

The following steps helped me transform and develop a relentless mindset which hardened me up mentally. While the old me would seek comfort: do the least amount of work possible and avoid contribution; I now welcome any opportunity to be uncomfortable. It has been the most powerful way for me to grow and foster a mindset which I could only describe with one word: "RELENTLESS", through pain and suffering.

The first step for me was to clear the mental fog. I admit

I was a bit lost, I would look for things to occupy my time, to escape reality, and my weight was gaining at a rate much quicker than before, which I had put down to age.

The chance meeting with my long-time friend opened my eyes to Intermittent Fasting (IF). I had heard of it before, but was sceptical of the results. I had never met anyone who had transformed their body so dramatically doing it, but seeing my friend that day not only gave me all the proof I needed, but inspired me to try it for myself. It was exactly the answer I needed to help me find clarity; it's funny that these chance encounters happen right when you need it the most.

I started my IF journey that night and told myself "just focus on the process and don't put any pressure to see any immediate results." Education was key too. I wanted to know everything about IF, so I read articles and watched videos online, which lead to related topics, including Keto and the importance of exercise and the positive effects it had on the mind. I knew this stuff before, but didn't put too much emphasis on it, until now. This motivated me to double down on my diet, exercise and my morning routine was born.

I could feel the mental fog starting to clear and my weight was slowly dropping, however the biggest change was my energy levels. I decided to take it up another level and to do everything I hated doing, plus complete it all before my kids woke up.

These next steps became my morning routine: 4am

wake up, meditate for 20 mins, hydrate with a sprinkle of Himalayan pink salt, 40 mins core workout, sauna and a 4 min cold shower. I did this for about 5 months straight until I had to modify my routine to do it in the living room because my daughter was teething. By this time I was clocking up 2-3 hours of podcasts each day, being super active on LinkedIn and my weight had dropped almost 15kgs, around 19% of my original body weight. In 5 months.

My morning routine steadied my mental strength, and then made it stronger. I still get surprised at how far I can now push myself in the gym. My self talk is "OK I'm feeling pain. Is this just lactic acid or am I going to break something?" If it's lactic acid I keep pushing, otherwise I would do a drop set to failure. My pain threshold has gone next level. I can truly feel my mindset transforming and without a doubt, "RELENTLESS" is now part of my DNA.

If you are ever in a dark place, get support. You don't realize how important that is. Once you stabilize mentally, prepare to fall back down a few notches before truly hitting rock bottom, but this preparation is crucial to help you get out of your Winter and make sure that it is only temporary. At this point, find the inspiration within you to start working on you. Start with your health, your spiritual side, quieten your mind and just focus on the process each day on making marginal gains of improvement. One of my biggest inspirations during that dark period was David Goggins; his no BS approach to life was exactly what I needed. I no longer see failure as a bad thing. In fact, I plan for it and lots of it, as well as not chasing materialistic things but rather focus on making an impact.

Something that surprises people when I tell them, is that I give up part of my day to send voice messages, organize Skype/Zoom calls with the younger generation of professionals who reach out to me and I just give advice based on what I've experienced. It's one of those ways I like to give back and will continue to do so on LinkedIn.

I wish you all an abundant and joyful life and hope that my story will inspire or have a positive impact in some way. And remember, BE RELENTLESS.

Sparking from Jimmy's story and his generous kindness of sharing his wisdom with the youth, Aristotle had his opinion on this particual subject as well:

"All who have meditated on the art of inspiriting mankind came to understand that the fate of humanity is bounded to the education of the youth."

Following our compilation of high achievers and thought leaders in the world, we get to read the story Abhijit Chatterjee. Abhijit was born in India and recently made the step to the United States based on his profound ardor and enthusiasm to develop and optimize cloud-based solutions.

Connect with Abhijit on LinkedIn:

https://www.linkedin.com/in/abby-abhijit-chatterjee-87198457

Or via email:

abhijitchatterjee2@gmail.com

Life is worth suffering but more worthy of living!

By Abhijit Chetterjee

It's quite a statement to start with. I wouldn't have stated that if it wasn't my life! A simple middle-class Indian life might look like a normal one, but the inside roller coaster that a person has to endure is limitless. It's a similar kind of the unheard story of an ordinary man who always wondered and admired the mighty heroes, while never thought destiny would play a different game with him.

Everything started with a fight to be born out of countless sperms and joined the race of 7 billion people and more specifically to one of the most populous countries on this planet. The race is over normally after winning but in this case, it was a mere qualification. Have you ever come across any strange person who desperately wants to become master of all trades but ends up being master in none…well, that's me!

Let's welcome you to my life's journey. A simple, ordinary upbringing brimming with countless possibilities (as it was told) to achieve whatever I would want to desire. A normal computer science engineer with mere knowledge of computer operating and extensive knowledge and expertise in "Call of Duty" and "Need for Speed" thought he conquered the world even before entering the race of life. My first encounter with life was when I was in 3rd year. Playing "Call of Duty" at night and crossing another level as a tactical soldier – was my daily routine. It was just like another night but I felt a little different. My left eye turned completely hazy and it seemed I lost my vision for a fraction of second.

Next morning…another day…another adventure! But this morning was a bit different. My eye was completely fine from outside but I almost lost the vision. Taken to the doctor immediately, but thankfully the doctor assured nothing to worry about as its a minor infection! 1-week rest with some drops would do the healing work. Well…not so assuring or simple life is! It took an ugly turn after 2 weeks when vision didn't get restored rather started giving pain in the butt moments! Rushed to hospital and my destiny started revealing it's plan slowly. It was a rare disease of choroiditis which needed to be treated only with level 1 grade steroids as no standard medicine is known for the treatment! Took the dose straightaway 3 days and 3 nights in Hospital without understanding a single bit but being freaking traumatized.

2 months of bed rest and almost a failed semester gave me a real good taste of harsh reality of life. It was just a starting point where things started going haywire. The side effects of steroids were many and one of them being the sensitive skin and stomach ache. Not even a single day passed by where I didn't have suicidal thoughts not only because of the excruciating pain but also for the fake sympathies and the hidden smiles and smirks of so-called well-wishers.

Days went by and like millions of other Indians, I also passed the journey of theoretical engineering without any practical knowledge of my domain and as the obvious result, the companies respectfully showed me the door and certain times told me over the phone and emails. A nine months journey of hopelessness and severe depression of comparison with classmates led me into farther darkness which literally drowned me in my own shit!!

Landed up in a job with a basic minimum wage of a blue-collar employee and strived my way through just to end another day and not getting fired! 9 months it takes to come out of mother's womb and the same exact time it took for me to call it enough when torture became unbearable! It took me a while to understand the nuances of the atrocities of my life which I played a huge role intentionally or unintentionally by not being smart!!

Fast forward 2 years and I joined MBA – another smart move (or rather the only move) at the time of need. My small pond world of collided with the ocean and the Big Bang happened. Worked off my sweats (Cause I am not a man of much intelligence) and secured top rank and understood one thing – no organization gives a damn about marks!! Still got placed in a reputed organization and life took another turn.

Working 2 years and 3 months in the company made me realize about life more than ever. All our lives, we were told to be studious, studying hard to secure a good job but no one ever mentions what good really means! A job is merely a way for sustenance but how can it ever sustain a life!!!! Paying off my own loans and mitigating my liabilities felt like a winning streak for me. Our biggest mistake lies in our mind. It always tricks us to think either on the future or dwell on the past but never on the present! School, society, social circle, professional circle define what we are but never answer who and why of the part. The missing equation leaves our lives puzzled and heckled all the way through.

Accept it, admit it and work on it – that's what I have learned through my experience. Life is always a roller coaster and it is designed in such format for almost all of us. Rather than getting stuck into the blame game, accepting it can really become our tranquilizer. It has always paved my way through the darkest times of my life and it continues to do so. Life can throw your plans out of the window but that means it is making plans for yourself. I started writing out of boredom and a way to avoid my anxiety and insecurities and never have I ever imagined that writing would become such an integral part of my life. We all need to stop existing and start living and trust me the journey will be easier when you take a different perspective to approach your life.

'When life puts you in tough situations, don't say "why me", say "try me". – a quote of wisdom

- Abhijit Chatterjee

I am a voracious reader, a consultant by profession and a foodie by passion and a freelance writer by love. Love to introspect, understand and analyze the complexities and try to find out a simple way of the mess – that's me!

No matter what happens in life, life goes on and the next peak has just started to ascend. The journey is what is important and we enjoy it by acknowledging the words of Mary Kay Ash:

" Imagine that every single person you meet has a his or her neck, saying 'Make me feel important!'
Not only will you succeed in sales, you will also succeed in life."

One person, who is truly following this advice is Dave Travolta. Dave is not just making an amazing closing to this first update to this extraordinary compilation of the brilliant bookwriters collective, he also shares something magnificent, which enlivens you and your heart with a truly courageous insight to life.

Reach out and say "Hi Brother" to Dave on his LinkedIn-Profile:
https://www.linkedin.com/in/davetravolta

The action is yours, when you take it.

By Dave Travolta

Hi. I am Dave and I am very happy to be part of this masterpiece of my friend Sascha. I took action towards writing a chapter in this book, as he approached me and asked me for my opinion. I was not sure, but I took action anyway. I listen to my inner voice and this is my intuition that shows me, what to do or what not to do. And I believe that this book and initiative is a great value to the people. Too many of us have been or still procrastinate and loose balance in their lives. Simply taking action is already the solution to many problems. Basically I observe my thoughts and see either a problem or a solution. Most times I have to persuade myself into taking action by visualising a certain outcome to motivate myself. Sometimes the right tasks pop up mentally and I just go for it. Neither do I think too much about my thoughts, nor do I procrastinate towards anxiety and stop doing things at all. I just love to take action and see my life getting fulfilled from all sides because I just allow things to happen with my influence.

For 26 years I had chronic inflammation of my skin, very bad ekcema and a lack of energy. I was following through all the suggestions and commands of my doctors and there was never a remedy, just dealing with symptoms. Today I know, that my way out of that was taking action on my own thoughts. I bought books, read thousands of pages and took action on what I have just learned. Knowing is not enough, we have to apply the things we learn to create the wisdom in the world and to be the change we want to see.

In the past I have been just thinking about taking action and how cool it would be, to have done this or that, and at the end, I suffered a lot of mental pain, because I did not take action towards what I really wanted. I did listen to the voice that told me stupid and bullshit stories about what might go wrong or what might happen in a bad way. I was considered to have the most pleasure of my life, but I never stepped into that potential, because the illusion was holding me back. The problem was that I was just thinking and not taking action while thinking. The key for me now is to see opportunities and if I don't see them, I create them. I observe other people around me and how they take action and it is not a big deal. It is actually very easy to think and follow through. It is easy to gain experience by just doing and not thinking about anything. I realize that it is about letting go of judgement and the result or outcome. I know that I will succeed and get what I want or where I want to be, because of just following my intentions. The act itself of taking action is nothing more than just 1 part of the process. If you want to get somewhere you need to start where you are and not where you might be. Many people do it the opposite way.

The most growth I see in my life is when I take action to the uncomfortable things. Things like important, but hurtful conversations with family, friends, co-workers or bosses. Even I see my progress best when I take action on topics I normally fear the most. I had to deal with approaching anxiety in my past. Not only with women, but with all people in general. I was shutting myself down, thinking too much about what could go wrong and did not see the chance to grow at all. Over the course of some time and repetition of the negative behaviour   it   got   even   worse.

How did I got out of that?

It took action. I simply forced myself to just say "Hi" to anybody. And do not allow the fear to overcome me in a bad way and instead see through the message. Because fear shows me the thing I really need to do to get where I want to be. So the more I was doing that, the more I learned, that other people have fears too and they have actually no idea how to deal with that too. So I shifted my perspective and became the person that helps people to grow, by positioning myself in the right way. I am still fearful sometimes, but I do not define myself with the fear, but more with the result that creates it when I DO NOT take action for better. If I just let my fear be there, it will create exact this and I do not get any results at all, except pain, suffering and more anxiety. And on top of that, I have to deal with the stress of losing opportunities,   chances   and   so   much   more.

I now know, that life is happening anyway, even without me taking action. The problem is, that other people will take action on me and with me and use me to get where they want to be, if I allow it to happen. I realize that with my power of choice: If I do not choose to take action, someone else will, and give me reasons to take action for their ideas.

Alright, this has been the first update to this amazing compendium! Brilliant and versatile stories have been shared - all unique, as life is.

We like to close this chapter with the assurance of more to come with this suiting quote:

"Everything starts with a first step. We reach our ideal by continuously improving our present situation with this one next action, action by action, step by step, step by step and surprise! We are, where we anticipated to be."

- The bookwriters collective

Outroduction

Dear Reader,

It has been a pleasure for all of us to write about this topic.

As you can see, "Taking Action!" goes very well in our favour and uplifts our quality of life.

If you take one idea from this book, make it the encouragement of saying "YES!" to your dreams, believing them to be possible and acting on them, in order to make them real.

When you like or love what you were reading, reach out to us! We are so happy about every connection and are eager to 'Take Action !' together. Keep in mind:

"You never truly know, until you do it."

Especially beneficial and appreciative to us is, when you leave a short uplifting review on your page of purchase or on amazon.

Amazon Link: https://amzn.to/2xZrBIU

We are so grateful for your time and send you our best greetings.

May you and your family be blessed.

The bookwriters collective

Disclaimer of liability

You are welcome to share this book with as many people as possible. Talk about it, remember the most inspiring ideas and enjoy your great life.

Impressum

Nino Anders
Papyrus Autoren-Club
R.O.M. Logicware GmbH
Pettenkoferstr. 16-18
10247 Berlin

www.ingramcontent.com/pod-product-compliance
Lightning Source LLC
Chambersburg PA
CBHW051223250726
48655CB00006B/2561